DIY
SURVIVAL
MANUAL

D0314824

NATURAL DISASTERS
AVOID ESCAPE SURVIVE

BEN HUBBARD

CARLTON
KiDS

THIS IS A CARLTON BOOK
Text, design and illustration © Carlton Books Limited 2019

Published in 2019 by Carlton Books Limited,
an imprint of the Carlton Publishing Group,
20 Mortimer Street, London W1T 3JW

A catalogue record for this book is available from the British Library.

ISBN: 978-1-78312-476-3
Printed in China

Design: Jake da'Costa and WildPixel Ltd.

The publishers would like to thank the following sources for their kind permission
to reproduce the pictures in the book.
t = top; b = bottom; c = centre; l = left; r = right

Pages 6–7, 52b spaxlax/Shutterstock, Rocksweeper/Shutterstock; 8–9 Visual Intermezzo/
Shutterstock; 11 Binaya Mangrati/Shutterstock; 12 Dolly MJ/Shutterstock, Arturo Limon/
Shutterstock, anaken2012/Shutterstock, Guzel Studio/Shutterstock, Africa studio/
Shutterstock, Elnur/Shutterstock; 13t Jason Stitt/Shutterstock; 13b maroke/Shutterstock;
14 polkadot_photo/Shutterstock, Africa studio/Shutterstock, Still AB/Shutterstock, Gaby
Koojiman/Shutterstock, Halfpoint/Shutterstock; 15tr Digital mammoth/Shutterstock;
16 Vladimir Mulder/Shutterstock; 17t Kleber Cordeir/Shutterstock; 17tr, 35bl, 37tr, 45tl, 53br,
69tl, 77tr, 85b & 101l Mega Pixel/Shutterstock; 17b Narongsak Nagadhana/Shutterstock;
18–19 Lysogor Roman/Shutterstock; 21tr Alex Egorov/Shutterstock; 22c Jakub Zak/
Shutterstock; 23c Cegli/Shutterstock; 23c Cegli/Shutterstock; 25c Musadeq Sadeq/AP/
REX/Shutterstock; 26c Mikhail Hoboton Popov/Shutterstock; 28–29 SeanRayford/Stringer/
Getty Images; 30c November27/Shutterstock; 30b 2M media/Shutterstock; 32t Pavel 1964/
Shutterstock; 33b travelview/Shutterstock; 34 MilanMarkovic78/Shutterstock; 35br mdm7807/
Shutterstock; 37t IrinaK/Shutterstock; 38–39 Smelov/Shutterstock; 41b Maridav/Shutterstock;
42t AFP/Stringer/Getty Images; 43tr Yvonne Bauer/Shutterstock; 45tr Giannis Papanikos/
Shutterstock; 46–47, 52c Bignai/Shutterstock; 48b Stocktrek/Getty Images; 50t Joey Santini/
Shutterstock; 51b sezer66/Shutterstock; 53bl Smallcreative/Shutterstock; 54–55,
60t sdecoret/Shutterstock; 56 elRoce/Shutterstock; 57t Martin Haas/Shutterstock;
58t Vincent noel/Shutterstock; 58b Africa studio/Shutterstock; 59t Martin Allinger/
Shutterstock; 59b Ranta Images/Shutterstock; 60 Susan Schmitz/Shutterstock, CREATISTA/
Shutterstock, Photo_ms/Shutterstock; 61 Minerva Studio/Shutterstock; 62–63, 68c Christian
Roberts-Olsen/Shutterstock; 64t Naoto Shinkai/Shutterstock; 64b yelantsevv/Shutterstock;
65 Colin Dewar/Shutterstock; 66t Smileus/Shutterstock, dovla/Shutterstock; 66b Serfey
Mironov/Shutterstock; 67tl AJR_photo/Shutterstock, 67tr bokan/Shutterstock; 67b Omeer/
Shutterstock; 68 Sergio Delle Vedouve/Shutterstock; 69tr Noah Bergeri/AP/REX/Shutterstock;
69b Sarah Jessup/Shutterstock; 70–71, 76c Warren Faidley/Getty Images; 74b Lisa F Young/
Shutterstock; 76b maroke/Shutterstock, Vladimirs Koskins/Shutterstock; 77tl Nathan Holland/
Shutterstock; 78–79 vitec/Shutterstock; 80t Frederic Legrand-COMEO/Shutterstock; 81t Ross
Ellet/Shutterstock; 85t Images & Stories/Alamy; 86–87, 92c Thomas Dekiere/Shutterstock;
88 Kletr/Shutterstock; 89t Dmytro Vietrov; 89c Great Sibera Studio/Shutterstock;
89br Jack Smith/AP/REX/Shutterstock; 91t Andalou Agency/Getty Images; 91b Alohaflamingo/
Shutterstock; 92 Axel Bueckert/Shutterstock; 93b Hysteria/Shutterstock; 93b Jurik Peter/
Shutterstock; 94–95 Tom Wang/Shutterstock; 97 Alexander Sherstobitov/Shutterstock;
99b Dean Drobert/Shutterstock; 100 Andrev_Popov/Shutterstock; 101r Marcio Jose Bastos
Silva/Shutterstock; 102–103 idiz/Shutterstock; 104 montree hanlue/Shutterstock; 106t Denis
Pogostin/Shutterstock; 107b Good Luck Photo/Shutterstock; 109 ExpediTom/Shutterstock;
109b creativesunday/Shutterstock.

DIY SURVIVAL MANUAL

NATURAL DISASTERS

AVOID ESCAPE SURVIVE

BEN HUBBARD

CARLTON KiDS

CONTENTS

INTRODUCTION

Have you ever been stuck on a seashore as a series of tsunami waves speed towards you? Has an avalanche ever swept you down a slope and buried you under several metres of snow? Has a hurricane ever ripped off the roof of your house, flooded it with water and left you for dead?

If the answer is yes, then congratulations, you are a natural born survivor (and perhaps a bit disaster prone)! For everyone else, don't worry: this manual will turn you into a serious Do It Yourself (DIY) survivor specialist. The following pages will cover all the major natural disasters, why they form, how to prepare for one, and what to do to survive.

Are you experiencing a natural disaster now and don't have time for all the reading? Then turn directly to the 'survive' pages of each section. This will give you on-the-spot advice for how to stay alive, thrive and come out smiling on the other side. So read on to learn how to evade earthquakes, outlast landslides, dodge droughts and withstand wildfires. Become a DIY survivalist now!

EARTHQUAKES

An earthquake is the sudden, violent shaking of the Earth's surface. Large earthquakes can crack open the ground, bring down buildings and reduce whole cities to rubble. They are among the most extreme natural disasters in the world. Worse still, earthquakes are impossible to predict or prevent.

Tell me about earthquakes

WHAT MAKES AN EARTHQUAKE?

We all know earthquakes can shake the ground and move it up, down and sideways. But what causes them to form in the first place?

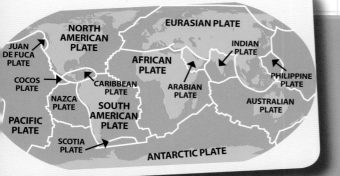

There are seven major tectonic plates on Earth and several minor ones.

EARTHQUAKE FORMING

The Earth's surface, or crust, is covered with giant slabs of rock called tectonic plates. These plates are constantly moving. When two plates grind past each other they release powerful waves of energy. These 'seismic' waves travel through the ground and make it shake. This shaking is what we know as an earthquake.

INSIDE A QUAKE

The exact point an earthquake begins is known as the focus. Here, the ground ruptures and seismic waves are sent out in every direction, like ripples on a pond. The seismic waves are felt most strongly at a point directly above the focus on the surface. This is called the epicentre.

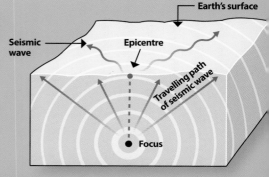

TYPES OF WAVES

The first waves to strike are called Primary, or P-waves. P-waves can travel through rock at speeds of 8 km/sec (5 mi./sec) and often cause cracks in the ground. Secondary, or S-waves, are slower than P-waves, but far more destructive. S-waves shake the ground up, down and sideways, which is the motion that brings buildings down.

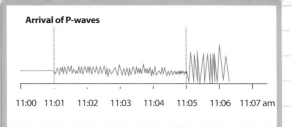

Arrival of P-waves

11:00　11:01　11:02　11:03　11:04　11:05　11:06　11:07 am

Scientists use seismometers to measure the strength of P-waves and S-waves. The results are shown in a seismograph, like this one.

EARTHQUAKE STRENGTH

The Moment Magnitude Scale records an earthquake's strength based on measurements of its seismic waves.

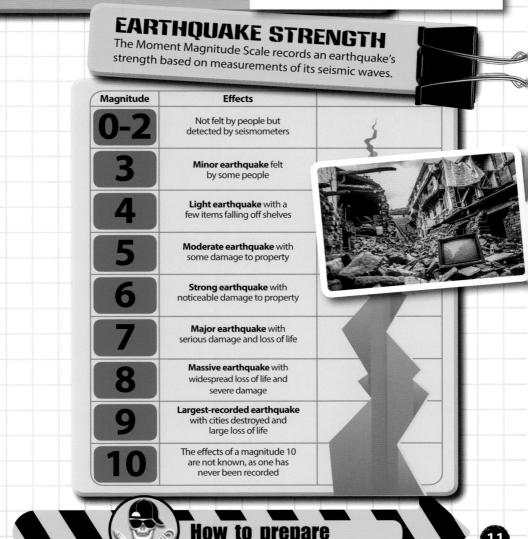

Magnitude	Effects
0-2	Not felt by people but detected by seismometers
3	**Minor earthquake** felt by some people
4	**Light earthquake** with a few items falling off shelves
5	**Moderate earthquake** with some damage to property
6	**Strong earthquake** with noticeable damage to property
7	**Major earthquake** with serious damage and loss of life
8	**Massive earthquake** with widespread loss of life and severe damage
9	**Largest-recorded earthquake** with cities destroyed and large loss of life
10	The effects of a magnitude 10 are not known, as one has never been recorded

How to prepare

HOW TO PREPARE

GET EMERGENCY KIT READY

Large earthquakes can mean surviving alone for several days without food, water or electricity. Having an emergency kit can be the difference between life and death. It should include:

- **Large bottles of water for drinking and sanitation**

- **Dried and tinned food to last for several days or more, with a tin opener**

- **Battery-powered radio**

- **Torch and extra batteries**

- **First aid kit**

- **Whistles to signal for help**

- **Mobile phone with extra batteries**

- **Toilet paper, plastic bags and duct tape to use as makeshift toilets.**

STEP 2

EARTHQUAKE-PROOF YOUR HOME

Move your bed away from windows. Put hooks over cupboard doors to stop them being shaken open. Move heavy and breakable items to lower shelves.

STEP 3

HAVE A PLAN

Know where to go and what to do when an earthquake strikes. Have somewhere to shelter under in each room, such as a table. Practise an earthquake drill with your family.

HOW TO SURVIVE

The ground is shaking, windows are rattling and glasses are smashing on the floor. It's an earthquake! What should you do?

SURVIVE STEP-BY-STEP

Earthquakes come without warning at any time of day or night. But wherever you are when an earthquake strikes, the advice is the same: DROP, find COVER and HOLD ON.

1 DROP: Copy your cat and drop onto all fours. This will make it easier to crawl to safety as the ground shakes around you.

2 COVER: If inside, find cover to protect yourself from falling debris. This can include walls, roofs or heavy objects on high shelves. A sturdy table can provide cover. If outside, move away from buildings, trees and powerlines.

3 HOLD ON: If you are under cover such as a table, hold onto one of its legs. This will keep you underneath it if it moves.

monster catfish

MYTH-BUSTING!

In ancient times, people believed earthquakes were caused by grumpy gods and monster catfish. Many myths and misconceptions about earthquakes remain today. Here are some of them:

Earthquakes are becoming more frequent.

Actually, instances of magnitude 7 earthquakes have remained constant for many years. All that has changed is the increase in instruments that record earthquakes.

The safest place to shelter is under a doorway.

In reality a doorway is no stronger than the rest of the building. In an earthquake, a door can also swing wildly and knock you out. Sheltering under a table or against an interior wall is best.

Earthquakes occur during calm 'earthquake weather'.

Not true: earthquakes happen deep inside the Earth at any time, in any weather.

EARTHQUAKE AREAS

Earthquakes can happen anywhere, but 90 per cent of them occur along the 'Ring of Fire' around the Pacific Ocean. This is a 40,000 km (25,000 mi.) zone where the large Pacific Plate meets several other tectonic plates. This causes many cracks in the Earth's crust where magma can reach the surface and erupt as volcanoes.

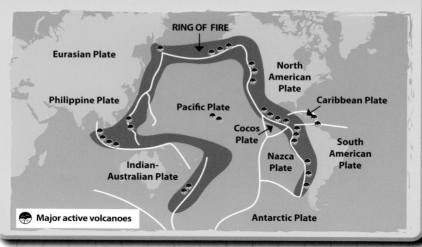

RING OF FIRE

Eurasian Plate

North American Plate

Philippine Plate

Caribbean Plate

Pacific Plate

Cocos Plate

South American Plate

Nazca Plate

Indian-Australian Plate

Antarctic Plate

Major active volcanoes

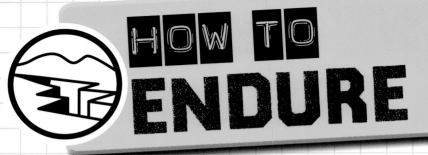

HOW TO ENDURE

Ok, so you've survived the quake and the shaking's stopped. But you're trapped beneath rubble. Now what?

HELP, I'M FREAKING OUT!

Being buried by earthquake rubble is a terrifying experience. You may be injured, have little air to breathe, and no food or water. First, keep calm and preserve your air supply by taking deep, slow breaths. Now, follow these steps:

 1 Cover your nose and mouth with clothing to avoid breathing in dangerous particles.

 2 Tap on pipes to call for help, or yell if you hear people above you.

3 If you have a mobile phone send text messages rather than calling to save on battery life.

 4 Stay positive. Remember, in 2005 a woman in Pakistan survived for 63 days under earthquake rubble by drinking rainwater.

TEST YOUR MATES

Now you're earthquake aware and ready for the big one. But what about your mates? Are they experts or earthquake amateurs? Test their knowledge with this true or false quiz.

A A magnitude 8 earthquake is 10 times stronger than a magnitude 7. **T/F**

B Stairways are a good place to shelter during a quake. **T/F**

C Aftershocks are uncommon after a big earthquake. **T/F**

D Most people die by being swallowed up by the ground during an earthquake. **T/F**

E There are over 500,000 earthquakes every year. **T/F**

F Dogs can detect earthquakes hours before they happen. **T/F**

G As far as we know, there has never been a magnitude 10 earthquake. **T/F**

Answers are at the back of the book

AVALANCHES

An avalanche is a mass of ice and snow that slides suddenly down a mountainside. Avalanches can travel at speeds of over 320 km/h (200 mph) and sweep away everything in their path. A powerful avalanche can knock over trees, cover buildings and bury people beneath several metres of snow.

Tell me about avalanches

An avalanche can occur anywhere there is snow, a slope and something to trigger it. So how do these things form an avalanche?

SNOWPACK LAYERS

Layers of snow are called snowpacks. Each layer contains a different kind of snow which has been formed during particular weather. When layers of thin, weak snow are positioned between layers of hard, icy snow, an avalanche becomes likely.

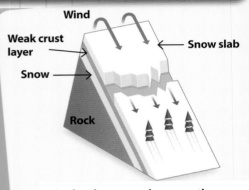

Wind

Weak crust layer

Snow slab

Snow

Rock

Avalanche-prone slopes are those with layers of different kinds of snow.

TYPES OF AVALANCHE

There are two main types of avalanche: powder and slab. Powdered snow is made up of snowflakes that do not bond together. When this weak snow lies on top of a layer of hard, icy snow it can easily become an avalanche. A slab avalanche is made up of a layer of weak snow covered by a layer of new snow. If a trigger causes the weak layer beneath to break, the top layer slides downwards as a slab.

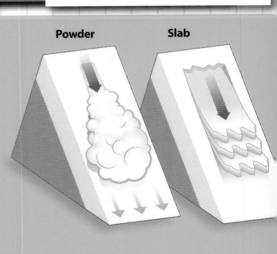

Powder

Slab

WHAT TRIGGERS AN AVALANCHE?

Avalanches are triggered by heavy snowfall, rain, wind, earthquakes, volcanoes and human activity. Someone walking, skiing or riding a snowmobile across a slope can trigger an avalanche.

Humans are often the main cause of avalanches on popular mountainsides.

AVALANCHE POINTS

An avalanche begins at the starting zone at the top of a slope, where unstable snow first breaks loose. As it rushes down a path known as the track, the avalanche collects snow, ice and rocks. The avalanche crashes to an end at the runout zone, at the bottom.

Starting zone

Track

Runout zone

How to prepare

HOW TO PREPARE

The best way to prepare for avalanches is to avoid them altogether. Do this by listening to avalanche warnings on the radio and avoiding avalanche-prone slopes. If you're out on a snowy mountain, make sure to carry an avalanche survival kit.

AVOID AN AVALANCHE

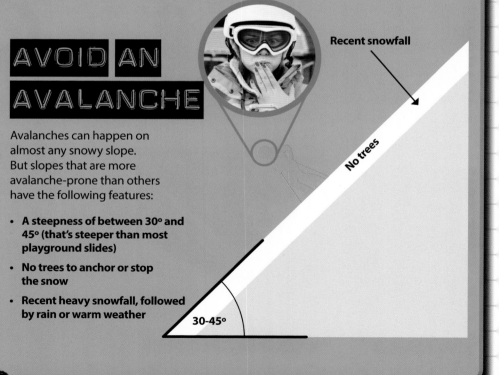

Avalanches can happen on almost any snowy slope. But slopes that are more avalanche-prone than others have the following features:

- A steepness of between 30° and 45° (that's steeper than most playground slides)

- No trees to anchor or stop the snow

- Recent heavy snowfall, followed by rain or warm weather

Recent snowfall

No trees

30-45°

AVALANCHE SURVIVAL KIT

Anyone hitting the powder needs a survival kit. Here's the low-down on what you need and why.

An avalanche transceiver sends out an electronic signal from your location if you're buried under snow. It can also receive the signals from other transceivers.

A probe is an extendable metal pole that can be pushed through the snow to the surface. This shows rescuers your exact location.

Use a folding avalanche shovel to dig yourself or your mates out of the snow.

How to survive

HOW TO SURVIVE

You've done your best to avoid triggering an avalanche. But suddenly there is movement from the slope above. A mass of white snow is sliding downwards, and it's getting faster and faster. Uh-oh! What now?

SURVIVE STEP-BY-STEP

1 Try and get above the sliding avalanche snow by moving quickly to the nearest ridge.

2 If you cannot get above the avalanche, get behind the nearest piece of hard cover like a rock or tree. This will help protect you.

3 If the avalanche catches you, try to keep your head above the snow.

4 If the avalanche is carrying you down the slope, try 'swimming' to the top of the snow.

CAN I CROSS?

Crossing an avalanche-prone slope is always a risk. But sometimes it's unavoidable. To improve your chances, move your rucksack onto one shoulder so you can easily drop it if needed. Now, begin treading gently, carefully and quickly across the slope. Stay light and nimble like a cat.

CASE STUDY

On February 9, 2010, over 165 people died in a series of avalanches that struck the Salang Pass in the Hindu Kush mountains, Afghanistan. The avalanches were triggered by extreme rainfall and high winds, which set large slabs of snow loose. Hundreds of motorists were left trapped in their vehicles as the avalanche plunged down from the mountainside above them. Heavy machinery was needed to dig the motorists out, but it arrived too late for many of them.

HOW TO ENDURE

The avalanche has caught you! You've been tossed about like a towel in a tumble dryer and dumped at the slope bottom under several metres of snow. Here, it's pitch black and the snow is muffling your screams. Worse still, it's becoming hard to breathe. Help!

HELP, I'M FREAKING OUT!

1 Make an air pocket around your head so you have room to breathe. Spitting against the snow can help with this. Work fast before the snow hardens.

2 Turn on your transceiver if you have one.

3 Find out where the surface is, by dribbling or peeing. Dribble and pee always travel downwards, so the opposite way is up to the surface.

4 Push your avalanche pole towards the surface.

5 Stay calm. Panicking will shorten your breath and reduce your chances of survival. Breathe slowly and evenly and begin digging upwards.

SURVIVOR ACCOUNT

In 1985, an American gold miner survived for 22 hours after being buried by snow. Lester J. Morlang burrowed through over 18 m (60 ft.) of snow to the surface after an avalanche struck the Bessie G. Mine on Snowstorm Mountain, Colorado. Morlang survived the ordeal because he had an air pocket around him. Unfortunately his colleague, who did not have an air pocket, perished in the disaster.

TEST YOUR MATES

You may now be an avalanche expert, but what about your mates? Are they avalanche survivors or suckers? Test their knowledge with this true or false quiz.

A After 15 minutes of being buried, an avalanche victim's chance of surviving is 90 per cent. **T/F**

B After 30 minutes of being buried, an avalanche victim's chance of surviving is 45 per cent. **T/F**

C Noises such as shouts or gunshots can trigger an avalanche. **T/F**

D Lack of oxygen rather than cold is more likely to kill avalanche victims. **T/F**

E Avalanches that kill humans are rarely caused by the people themselves. **T/F**

F Around 25 per cent of those killed in avalanches die from being tossed into an obstacle such as a tree or rock. **T/F**

Answers are at the back of the book

FLASH FLOODS

Flash floods are deadly weather disasters that strike without warning. A flash flood can burst the banks of a river, wash away vehicles and leave whole towns swamped with water. Many people lose their lives in flash floods every year.

195

Tell me about flash floods

WHAT MAKES A FLASH FLOOD?

Flash floods are unpredictable disasters that quickly become dangerous. Even 15 cm (6 in.) of fast-moving floodwater can knock a person off their feet. So why does a flash flood form?

FLASH FLOOD FORMING

Flash floods can be caused by a dam failing or the sudden melting of snow. Often, however, a flash flood forms after heavy rainfall. Sometimes the rain falls on saturated ground that cannot take more water. At other times, rainwater runs over the top of dry, hard ground that cannot soak it up. Torrential rainfall can also cause rivers to rise and overflow, or break their banks.

Floodwater running over dry, hard ground in Chiang Rai, Thailand in 2015.

Small areas such as basements can fill quickly with water and become a life-threatening hazard.

TOWNS AND CITIES

Flash floods often occur in towns and cities when drainage systems become blocked or can't cope with the sudden deluge of water. This can cause streets, homes and buildings to be suddenly struck with rapidly rising water. When this happens, underground car parks, basements and underpasses can all become death traps.

RIVER VALLEYS

Flash floods can pose a great danger for villages and towns situated in river valleys. Floods here occur when water runs down over already saturated slopes into the valley below. The ground at the bottom is usually also saturated and so the water rises. If the local river then bursts its banks or spills over, a flooding disaster follows.

1. Heavy rain falls on to waterlogged ground.

2. Rainfall cannot soak in so runs down into the river.

3. River rises dramatically and bursts its banks flooding the valley floor.

FLASH FLOOD FAST FACTS

- Flash floods usually take place over a three to six hour period.

- Over half of flash flood fatalities occur when people are swept away in their cars.

- In the United States, more people die in flash floods than tornadoes and hurricanes.

- Just 60 cm (23 in.) of fast-moving floodwater can carry away a car.

60 cm (23 in.)

How to prepare

HOW TO PREPARE

Following these steps can help you prepare as much as possible for the deluge.

STEP 1

PROTECT YOUR HOME

Place sandbags around all exterior doors to your home. Turn off the electricity and gas at the mains. Move valuable items to the highest possible place.

STEP 2

CREATE A FLOOD KIT

- battery-powered radio
- tinned food and water
- first aid kit
- torch
- mobile phone
- extra batteries
- spare keys to your home
- dry clothes
- wet weather gear
- waterproof plastic covers for important documents

STEP 3

LISTEN TO THE NEWS

News broadcasts will keep you updated about approaching floodwaters, whether help is on the way and if you should evacuate your home.

STEP 4

STAY PUT, PET

Make sure your pets are with you and not able to run away when the flood arrives. Put your cat into a carrier with blankets inside if it becomes jittery.

HOW TO SURVIVE

A flash flood has caught you by surprise. The waters are rising fast, you're getting worried and your feet are wet! What should you do?

SURVIVE STEP-BY-STEP

If you find yourself swept away by floodwaters, don't panic and follow these instructions.

1 Try to stay on your back so you can go over obstacles and not underneath them.

2 Grab a large piece of floating debris if you can and keep your feet pointed downstream.

3 Hold an arm out of the water and yell loudly until someone comes to help.

SURVIVE STEP-BY-STEP

Your family has tried to flee a flash flood by car, but the waters have washed you off the road. Now your car is filling with water. What should you do? Follow these tips to survive:

1 Open all the windows and unlock the doors. If your car becomes submerged, the pressure of the water will make it impossible to open the doors and windows and you'll be trapped inside.

2 Release your seatbelts. These can keep you trapped in a flooding car.

3 Swim from the car before it completely fills with water. Hold on to something that floats, if you have it.

CASE STUDY

In 2013, a series of flash floods claimed the lives of 101 people in Argentina. The floods were caused by over 40 cm (16 in.) of rainfall, which fell in just two hours. In the cities of La Plata and Buenos Aires, over 3,000 people were evacuated from their homes and thousands stranded on rooftops as the floodwaters rapidly rose. Most of those killed were elderly people who became trapped inside. Later it was found that the cities' drainage systems could not cope with the sudden deluge of water.

HOW TO ENDURE

Flash floods strike suddenly but their effects can last for a long time. Some flooded regions remain under water for days or weeks afterwards. This is also when flash flood survivalists need to be at their most cautious.

HELP, I'M FREAKING OUT!

Don't panic and follow these top ten tips to help keep you safe.

 1 Floodwater is often contaminated with sewage. Make sure to wash your hands and disinfect anything that gets wet.

 2 Avoid fast flowing water wherever possible: floodwater is often stronger than it looks.

3 If you have to cross a flooded road, cross at the shallowest point and use a stick to probe for deep spots.

 4 Do not move through water with downed power lines: these could give you a deadly shock.

 5 Don't drink any water unless it has come out of a bottle. Boil tap water if there is no alternative.

 6 Don't eat food that has become wet.

 7 Make sure pets are kept above the flood water.

 8 Don't use electrical equipment until the plugs have been tested for safety.

 9 Don't leave your home until you have had the all-clear from local authorities.

10 Listen to radio reports for advice and instructions.

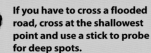

SURVIVOR ACCOUNT

Jessica Richard was one of thousands of residents stranded when a flash flood struck her home in Houston, Texas in 2017. The flood was caused by Hurricane Harvey, which brought torrential rainfall to the area. Nearly one million people left their homes as water spilled over from local rivers and reservoirs. Richard said her family was caught in waist-high water, which contained both snakes and spiders, before they were rescued from their home.

TEST YOUR MATES

Now you're ready to endure any type of flash flood: inside, outside, or in your car. But what about your mates? Do they have survivor flair or are they flash flood fools? Test them with this true or false quiz.

A Floodwaters commonly travel at a speed of 3 m (9 ft.) per second. **T/F**

B A large flash flood is believed to have wiped out all life on Mars. **T/F**

C Flash floods can take place in the desert. **T/F**

D Flash floods cannot rip away large bridges. **T/F**

E Most people who die in flash floods are caught trying to flee the water. **T/F**

F One of history's deadliest flash floods hit China in 1931. Between 400,000 and 4 million people died. **T/F**

Answers are at the back of the book

VOLCANOES

A volcano is an eruption of lava, ash and searing hot gas. Large volcanoes are the most powerful force in nature. They can explode with the strength of several nuclear bombs, bringing widespread destruction and great loss of life. Volcanoes kill hundreds of people every year – here's how to avoid being one of them.

VOLCANO TYPES

The shape of a volcano varies from a simple crack in the ground to familiar, cone-shaped mountains. These cone-shaped mountains are called composite volcanoes, or stratovolcanoes, and are formed from many layers of lava. The other three main types of volcanoes are: shield volcanoes, cinder cones and lava domes.

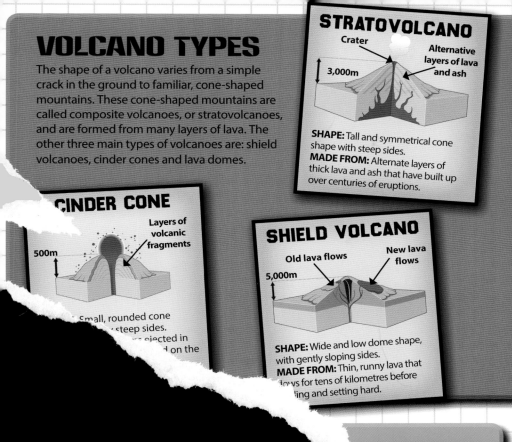

STRATOVOLCANO

Crater

Alternative layers of lava and ash

3,000m

SHAPE: Tall and symmetrical cone shape with steep sides.
MADE FROM: Alternate layers of thick lava and ash that have built up over centuries of eruptions.

CINDER CONE

Layers of volcanic fragments

500m

Small, rounded cone steep sides.
ejected in
on the

SHIELD VOLCANO

Old lava flows

New lava flows

5,000m

SHAPE: Wide and low dome shape, with gently sloping sides.
MADE FROM: Thin, runny lava that flows for tens of kilometres before ing and setting hard.

T SPOTS

argest volcanoes are formed when extra-hot magma punches a hole straight through a tectonic plate. These volcanoes are called hot spots. Hawaii's Kilauea is a hotspot volcano and one of the most active volcanoes in the world.

How to prepare

HOW TO PREPARE

Volcanic eruptions bring greater threats than just lava.
Here's how to identify and prepare for the main ones.

TAKE SHELTER

Know where the nearest shelter is to protect against projectiles. These are rocks hurled for kilometres into the air during an eruption. Some are as big as cars, but even a tennis-ball sized projectile will kill you.

BREATHE SAFELY

Buy a gas mask against the poisonous volcanic gases: carbon dioxide, sulphur dioxide and hydrogen sulphide. These gases can eat through clothes, burn eyes and cause suffocation.

CASE STUDY

In 79 AD, the volcano Mount Vesuvius erupted over the Roman cities of Pompeii and Herculaneum, in Naples, Italy. The eruption blackened the sky and pyroclastic flows killed over 2,000 people. The cities were then buried under 7 m (23 ft.) of volcanic debris until the 18th century. Then it was found the bodies of the dead had left 3D imprints in the volcanic debris. These imprints were filled with plaster to reveal models of the residents, huddling together and covering their faces in terror.

TEST YOUR MATES

? You're now a volcano wizard but what about your mates? Are they volcano experts or idiots? Test their knowledge with this true or false quiz.

A There are over 1,500 active volcanoes in the world. **T/F**

B Residents make up the largest number of volcano fatalities, followed by scientists, tourists and the media. **T/F**

C Earth is the only planet in our solar system where volcanoes are found. **T/F**

D The deadliest volcanic eruption since 1500 was Indonesia's Krakatoa, which killed over 36,000 people in 1883. **T/F**

Answers are at the back of the book

45

TSUNAMIS

A tsunami is a massive wave, or series of waves, that can wash away villages and leave whole cities devastated. Tsunami waves can reach 13 storeys high and travel at speeds of over 800 km/h (500 mph). When it reaches land, a tsunami can be an unstoppable wall of seawater that strikes with the force of concrete.

Tell me about tsunamis

WHAT MAKES A TSUNAMI?

Tsunamis begin in the deep ocean as small, 30 cm (1 ft.) high waves. But they can grow to over 40 m (131 ft.) by the time they hit the shore. So why do tsunamis form?

TSUNAMI FORMING

Tsunamis are often caused by undersea earthquakes. These earthquakes rupture the seabed, which pushes a great mass of water up and outwards. This water then becomes small waves, which pulse out in all directions. As they travel towards land, the waves can generate enough power to wash away anything in their path.

Series of low waves

Waves build in height

Sea level

Shallows

Shock waves

Tsunamis travel fastest in deep water. At a depth of 7,000 m (22,965 ft.), a tsunami can reach speeds of over 800 km/h (500 mph).

WAVE TRAINS

Before a tsunami strikes, it sucks out all the water on the shore before it. The weight of the water behind a tsunami makes it not only high, but powerful. A series of tsunami waves, known as a 'wave train', can sweep away cars and houses like driftwood. The debris-strewn waves can then travel for as far as 16 km (10 mi.) inland.

A 2011 tsunami devastated dwellings and travelled 10 km (6 mi.) inland across Japan's Sendai region.

OTHER CAUSES

Tsunamis are not only caused by earthquakes. Landslides from cliff faces, both by the shores of oceans and lakes, can cause a tsunami. Underwater volcanoes and asteroids from space can also cause tsunamis. An asteroid crashing into the Pacific Ocean 2.5 million years ago created a mega-tsunami that swept over parts of South America and Antarctica.

An illustration of the Eltanin asteroid hitting the ocean and causing a mega-tsunami

TSUNAMI TIDAL WAVE MYTH BUSTER

Tsunamis and tidal waves are often incorrectly believed to be the same thing. In reality, tsunamis are caused by earthquakes, underwater volcanoes and landslides. Tidal waves are caused by the gravitational pull of the Moon and Sun on the Earth's oceans.

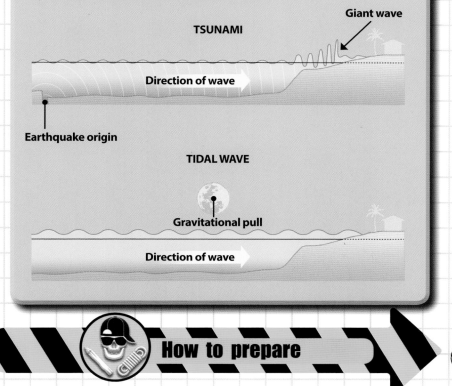

Giant wave

TSUNAMI

Direction of wave

Earthquake origin

TIDAL WAVE

Gravitational pull

Direction of wave

HOW TO PREPARE

There are several signs a tsunami is imminent. Any one of them means you must head for higher ground inland immediately! Stay alert for:

1 Tsunami watches on the radio and tsunami warning sirens along the shore. A watch means a tsunami may happen, a warning means one is on its way.

2 Small earthquakes or ground tremors. These often signal a tsunami is coming.

3

The tide drawing back suddenly to expose the shore and flapping fish.

4

A loud roaring noise coming from the deep ocean. This means the waves will soon be visible!

HOW TO SURVIVE

Uh-oh, there's trouble on the beach. The water has been sucked away from the shore and there's a sound like 100 jetplanes coming from the sea. What should you do?

SURVIVE STEP-BY-STEP

1 Drop anything unimportant and run inland. Get to 30 m (100 ft.) above sea level and 3.2 km (2 mi.) away from the shore.

2 If you cannot reach higher ground, the top storeys of high, reinforced-concrete hotels are the next best bet. If there are no buildings, climb a tree.

3 If you are caught in a tsunami wave, you cannot outswim it. Try instead to climb onto a large piece of floating debris, such as a door.

4 When you reach a place of safety, do not go back to the shore until the all-clear has been given. Many people survive the first tsunami wave, just to be caught by the second and third waves when they go back to have a look.

MYTH-BUSTING BOX

There are many myths and misconceptions about tsunamis. Here are some of the main ones:

People who die in tsunamis always drown.

Not true: many tsunami fatalities are caused by people being crushed against debris.

You can surf a tsunami wave.

In reality, tsunami waves are sometimes hundreds of kilometres long and often don't stack up like a breaking wave. It would be impossible to surf one.

If you see a tsunami wave it is too late.

It's true that few people could outrun a tsunami, but many could climb to the top of a tall tsunami tower after they saw the waves coming.

SURVIVOR ACCOUNT

In 2015, Jocelyn Tordecilla Jorquera was caught by a tsunami after a magnitude 8.3 earthquake struck the coast of her native Chile. "Out of my window I saw the sea start to rise extremely quickly and come crashing in about two metres high into the coastline…the force of the wave was enough to destroy the houses that are at sea level," Jorquera said. Luckily, the family escaped to a safe area 20 m (66 ft.) above sea level, but their home was badly damaged.

TORNADOES

A tornado is a powerful, spinning column of air that speeds across the ground and sucks up anything in its path. The winds of a tornado can snap tree trunks, toss trucks like toys, and flatten whole towns. Tornadoes are among nature's most violent and deadly storms.

Tell me about tornadoes

WHAT IS A TORNADO?

We know that tornadoes are like gigantic, funnel-shaped vacuum cleaners, but what exactly are they and how do these terrifying twisters form?

HOW A TORNADO FORMS

A tornado is formed inside a large thunderstorm cloud. These clouds are made from warm, moist air that rises from the ground and strikes cool air in the atmosphere. This causes the cloud to rotate. A tornado twists down from a rotating thunderstorm cloud and hits the ground, sucking up dust and debris. This gives a tornado its familiar black colour.

EYE OF THE STORM

Inside the fast-spinning winds of a tornado is a calm, quiet centre called its eye. Some people have even stood inside a tornado's eye. They say it is like being in a large pipe. Whirling around the eye are objects caught up in the tornado's destructive winds.

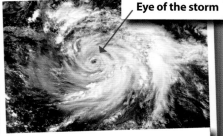

Eye of the storm

A satellite image of a tornado taken from space. You can see the eye of the storm at the centre.

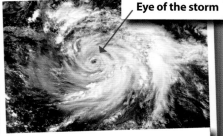

SPEEDS AND SIZES

A large tornado can be hundreds of metres wide and travel at a terrifying 96 km/h (60 mph). Inside them are the fastest winds ever recorded in nature. Some can reach 322 km/h (200 mph). This gives a large tornado a roaring sound like 100 jet engines.

Tornadoes are so powerful they can destroy houses and turn cars over.

TORNADO RATING SYSTEM

The Enhanced Fujita Scale measures the strength of a tornado based on the damage it has caused.

	Rating	Speed	Damage
	EF0	105–137 km/h (65–85 mph)	**MINOR DAMAGE:** tree branches broken, roofs peeled off
	EF1	138–177 km/h (86–110 mph)	**MODERATE DAMAGE:** windows broken, mobile homes overturned
	EF2	178–217 km/h (111–135 mph)	**CONSIDERABLE DAMAGE:** cars tossed, homes lifted off foundations
	EF3	218–265 km/h (136–165 mph)	**SEVERE DAMAGE:** significant damage to large buildings, parts of homes destroyed
	EF4	267–321 km/h (166–200 mph)	**EXTREME DAMAGE:** houses levelled, cars thrown significant distances
	EF5	322+ km/h (200+ mph)	**INCREDIBLE DAMAGE:** trees snapped, houses swept away, concrete buildings destroyed

How to prepare

HOW TO PREPARE

Tornadoes can be scary, but following these four steps can give you peace of mind.

STEP 1

SEEK SHELTER

Always know where to shelter before a tornado strikes. A specially built storm shelter, safe room, or underground basement is best.

STEP 2

SCAN THE NEWS

Radio and TV broadcasts give weather alerts and tornado warnings. A 'tornado emergency' means it's time to take shelter immediately.

STEP 3

WATCH THE WEATHER

Warning signs can include the sky turning a greenish-black colour, falling hail, or a sound like a waterfall.

STEP 4

LISTEN OUT

Many towns sound a loud siren as a tornado warning. This is your last chance to get to shelter. Do not get into a car or try to run if you hear a siren.

HOW TO SURVIVE

Ok, so you've been caught short. A tornado is travelling towards you and there's no shelter in sight. What do you do?

SURVIVE STEP-BY-STEP

1 Jump into a bathtub and cover yourself with cushions against falling debris. Bathtubs are often the only things left in place after a tornado strikes.

2 Get inside a closet, under the stairs, or beneath a heavy table. This will protect you if the walls and roof cave in.

3 If you are caught in the open and there is no rain, lie flat in a ditch or low area.

4 If there is rain, flash flooding may occur. Therefore, take shelter away from ditches, trees and powerlines. Crouch down and make yourself small.

5 Don't get into a car or mobile home, even if it is tempting. These are often the first objects to be thrown through the air by a tornado.

SURVIVOR ACCOUNT

In 2013, a tornado in Moore, Oklahoma, USA, demolished a hospital as Shay-la Taylor was inside giving birth. She describes the event: "The floor was shaking like an earthquake and then I saw the ceiling shaking too. Me and two of the nurses were all just holding hands. My eyes were closed, but you could kind of see daylight. And I opened my eyes and I could see out the wall." Incredibly, Taylor was unharmed and gave birth to a baby boy.

? TEST YOUR MATES

It is sometimes hard to believe the strange objects that have been sucked up by tornadoes. Can you and your mates guess which of the following are true or false?

A A tornado once tossed a grand piano nearly 400 m (1,310 ft.) through the air.　　　　**T/F**

B A tornado once picked up an 18-tonne (20-ton) truck and bounced it 300 m (985 ft.) down a motorway.　　　　**T/F**

C A tornado once sucked up a pond of frogs and rained them down on a nearby town.　　　　**T/F**

Answers are at the back of the book

WILDFIRES

Wildfires are fierce, unplanned fires that spread fast and burn through large areas of land. Wildfires can reach temperatures of 800°C (1,472°F), incinerate thousands of hectares of countryside and put people and property at serious risk. Thousands of people die in wildfires every year.

WILDFIRE WEATHER

Wildfires often follow a drought, heatwave or other period of hot weather with little rainfall. Strong winds can also contribute to a wildfire spreading. A weather cycle called El Niño brings strong, dry winds, which often feed wildfires in Australia.

In Australia, wildfires are called bushfires. A recent Australian bushfire is shown here.

FIRE TRIANGLE

Wildfires need three things to burn: heat, oxygen and fuel. Together, these elements are known as the 'fire triangle'. If one part of the triangle is removed, a wildfire cannot keep burning.

OXYGEN

HEAT

FUEL

How to prepare

65

HOW TO PREPARE

Follow these simple steps to keep you safe in the event of a wildfire.

STEP 1

READY YOUR HOME

Clear a 9 m (30 ft) space called a firebreak around your home, by removing dry leaves, timber, dead trees and anything else that could burn.

STEP 2

PREPARE YOUR GEAR

On top of a normal emergency kit (see pages 12–13), gather fire extinguishers, hosepipes, sprinklers and facemasks called 'particulate respirators' to cover your mouth and nose from smoke.

HAVE A PLAN

Have a fire drill that your whole family practises. That way, everyone knows where to go and what to do if smoke is seen nearby.

STEP 4

NEWS WARNINGS

Listen to the news for wildfire warnings during periods of hot, dry weather. Keep an eye out for signs of smoke, especially if you live in the countryside.

How to survive

HOW TO SURVIVE

The news is everywhere: a fast-moving wildfire is travelling in your direction. You can see smoke on the horizon and flames in the tops of trees. It's a deadly crown fire! What should you do?

SURVIVE STEP-BY-STEP

1 Close all the doors and windows in your home and set sprinklers going on the roof.

2 Turn on all the lights inside so the rooms will be visible in the smoke to firefighters.

3 If you are outside, move downhill towards water or a cleared area where there is little fuel for a fire to burn. Cover your head, mouth and nose with a mask or wet cloth.

4 If you are outside and surrounded by fire, dig a ditch and try and cover yourself with soil. This is only to be used in a worst case scenario!

5 If you are trapped in a car, roll up the windows, close the air vents, cover yourself with coats or blankets and crouch as low as possible.

CASE STUDY

In November 2018, the worst wildfire in California's history struck the American state. The so-called 'Camp Fire' killed at least 85 people, destroyed 14,000 homes and burned through over 153,000 acres of land. After 17 days of fighting the blaze, 1,000 firefighters were able to beat the fire back. Thousands of people were instantly made homeless and hundreds unaccounted for. High temperatures, gusty winds and vegetation contributed to the fire, which scientists say was the result of climate change.

TEST YOUR MATES

You may now be a wildfire expert, but what about your mates? Are they wildfire wizards or witless wonders? Test their knowledge with this true or false quiz.

A Smokejumpers are firefighters that parachute from planes to battle wildfires. **T/F**

B At any one time, there is a wildfire burning somewhere in the world. **T/F**

C Wildfires always travel downhill, not uphill. **T/F**

D Wildfires are never called bushfires, forest fires, hill fires and grass fires in different countries. **T/F**

E Wildfires can happen anywhere, but they frequently occur in the USA, Canada, Brazil and Australia. **T/F**

Answers are at the back of the book

HURRICANES

A hurricane is a swirling, super-charged thunderstorm that forms over warm seas before unleashing itself on shore. Once it hits land, a hurricane can contain winds of over 257 km/h (160 mph) and produce over 9 trillion litres (2.4 trillion gallons) of rain a day. This is why hurricanes are one of the most deadly and destructive natural disasters on Earth.

Tell me about hurricanes

WHAT MAKES A HURRICANE?

Hurricanes begin life as simple thunderstorms. However, not all thunderstorms turn into hurricanes. Conditions have to be perfect for one to form. Here's how it happens.

BIRTH OF A HURRICANE

Hurricanes are thunderstorms that suck up warm, moist air from the surface of tropical oceans. This creates a column of cloud, which then sucks in more air from around it. The air becomes wind, which rotates around a central point known as the storm's eye. When this rotating wind reaches 120 km/h (75 mph), the storm officially becomes a hurricane.

Water evaporates from the ocean surface and comes into contact with a mass of cold air, forming clouds.

A column of low pressure air develops at the centre. Winds form around the column.

As pressure in the central column (the eye) weakens, the speed of the wind around it increases.

FULLY FORMED

A fully-formed hurricane can contain storm clouds over 15,250 m (500,000 ft.) high and 200 km (125 mi.) across. As a hurricane travels across the water towards land, it becomes windier and more powerful. A hurricane is at its strongest when it first hits the shore.

Eye

A hurricane's eye alone can be 8–28 km (5–30 mi.) wide.

HURRICANE AREAS

Hurricanes typically take place over tropical regions, as shown on this map. Hurricanes have different names in different places: they are cyclones in the Indian Ocean, typhoons in the Pacific Ocean and hurricanes in the Atlantic Ocean.

Typhoons

Hurricanes

Cyclones

HURRICANE CATEGORIES

The Saffir-Simpson Hurricane Wind Scale gives a hurricane a 1–5 rating based on its wind speed and the damage it causes.

Category	Wind Speed	Damage	
1	119–153 km/h (74–95 mph)	**Dangerous winds** will produce some damage to homes. Tree branches will snap and power lines may be brought down.	
2	154–177 km/h (96–110 mph)	**Extremely dangerous** winds will uproot small trees, block roads and damage roofs. The power may be out for some weeks.	
3	178–208 km/h (111–129 mph)	**Devastating damage** will take place on house roofs and walls. Large trees will be snapped and uprooted.	
4	209–251 km/h (130–156 mph)	**Catastrophic damage** to houses and buildings. Most trees and power lines will be snapped. Power will be out for months.	
5	252 km/h + (157 mph) +	**Utterly catastrophic** damage to buildings and homes. Fallen trees and power lines will block access to residential areas, which will be uninhabitable for many months.	

How to prepare

HOW TO PREPARE

Don't let the thought of a hurricane send you into a spin – follow these simple steps to keep you safe.

STEP 1

LISTEN OUT

Listen to news broadcasts about approaching hurricanes. These may tell you to evacuate your home. This is especially important if you are near a river that can flood or in unstable accommodation like a caravan.

STEP 2

BOARD UP

If you are staying in your home, board up your windows and doors and make sure your pets are safely inside. Make sure you have an emergency kit (see pages 12–13).

STEP 3

STAY SAFE

Select a safe area in your home to ride out the hurricane. This should be near the centre of the house, away from windows and exterior doors.

STEP 4

STAY INSIDE

Stay inside until radio reports have given the all-clear, even if it sounds like the hurricane has passed. Sometimes this could just mean you are inside the eye of the hurricane, which can bring up to an hour of calm weather.

HOW TO SURVIVE

A Category 4 hurricane is battering your home. The walls are shaking, windows rattling and the roof sounds like it will be peeled away. Hold tight!

SURVIVE STEP-BY-STEP

1 Stay put in your safe area, even if you are freaking out. Get under a table if possible in case the roof or walls come down. Otherwise, lie on the floor.

2 If a pet escapes outside, don't chase it. It will have to look after itself and you can't risk losing your life in trying to find it.

3 If water starts to come in under doorways, turn off the electricity at the mains and move as high up as you can.

4 Stay away from electrical equipment and landline telephones during a hurricane as they can attract lightning and give you a shock.

5 Remember, the majority of people caught in a hurricane have lived to tell the tale. Keep calm, breathe evenly, stay sensible and wait for it to pass.

MYTH-BUSTING BOX

There are many myths and misconceptions about hurricanes. Below are some of the main ones:

Hurricane season usually runs from June to November.

This is only true if you're in the Northern Hemisphere. In the Southern Hemisphere, hurricane season is generally between November and April.

All hurricanes are named.

Actually, only hurricanes with winds that reach 62 km/h (39 mph) are officially named. Names are picked in advance and run in alphabetical order.

Hurricanes can travel for many miles inland.

This is incorrect. Once on land, a hurricane dies out quickly because it no longer has warm water to fuel it.

Even mildly warm seawater can power a hurricane.

Not true. Seawater has to have a temperature of at least 27°C (80°F) to be fuel for a hurricane.

Hurricane

Sea

Inland

77

BLIZZARDS

Blizzards are severe snowstorms that bring strong winds and blowing snow. One of nature's deadliest winter storms, a blizzard usually strikes unexpectedly and leaves people stranded in freezing, sub-zero conditions. Hundreds are caught out by blizzards every year.

Tell me about blizzards

WHAT MAKES A BLIZZARD?

Blizzards are not as common as other weather disasters such as snowstorms, tornadoes or hurricanes, but when they strike they almost always cause fatalities. So how does a blizzard form?

BLIZZARD TICKBOX

Every blizzard begins life as a snowstorm, but not every snowstorm becomes a blizzard. A snowstorm turns into a blizzard when it has:

- Violent winds of at least 56 km/h (35 mph) or more ✓

- Snow that greatly reduces visibility ✓

- A lifespan of three hours or more ✓

Blizzards commonly cause cars to come to a standstill because motorists cannot see through the snow to drive.

BLIZZARD TYPES

Blizzards typically blow about falling snow in violent gusts of winds. However, during a ground blizzard, there is no falling snow. Instead, the winds whip up the snow and ice already lying on the ground.

Ground blizzards are dangerous because they can occur after winter storms have passed and people are caught off guard.

BLIZZARD FORMING

Blizzards need the following winter weather conditions to form:

1. MOISTURE IN THE AIR (also called water vapour) to create clouds and snow.

2. COLD AIR (below freezing) at ground level and above in the clouds. This ensures falling snow does not turn into rain.

3. WARM AIR that rises over the cold air. This causes strong winds and snow to fall.

Warm air rises over the cold dome

Clouds and water vapour form

Dome of cold air

EFFECTS OF A BLIZZARD

Blizzards often cause havoc in urban areas and can bring whole cities to a standstill. The heavy snowfall can cut off electricity, cause roofs to cave-in and prevent vehicles from moving. Often, people are caught in their cars on roads for many hours when a blizzard unexpectedly strikes. Those trapped in cars or outside during a blizzard quickly become at risk of frostbite and hypothermia from the freezing cold.

How to prepare

HOW TO PREPARE

Brrr! It's getting colder outside. Follow these four steps to keep from freezing.

STEP 1

READY YOUR HOME

Stock up on food and water for your home at the start of winter before snowfall begins. Make sure you have an emergency kit (see pages 12–13).

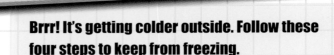

STEP 2

WEATHER WARNINGS

Listen to blizzard watches and warnings. If you are inside when a warning is issued, dress warmly, prepare for power outages and don't go outside.

STEP 3

WINTER WALKING

If you are spending time in the wilderness during winter, stay blizzard-ready by carrying a foldable shovel, thermal underwear, extra batteries for your mobile phone, dried food and water, and an avalanche transceiver (see pages 22–23).

STEP 4

CAR TRAVEL

If you are driving with your family during blizzard season, make sure your car has warm blankets, a windscreen scraper, a tow rope, food and water, a battery-powered radio and extra batteries for mobile phones.

☐ Get Vehicle Services
☐ Check Cooling System
☐ Check Battery
☐ Fill Washer Fluid
☐ Check Wipers & Defrosters
☐ Windshield for Rock Chips
☐ Inspect Tyre Tread & Age
☐ Check Belts & Hoses
☐ Check Lights
☐ Pack Emergency kit

How to survive

HOW TO SURVIVE

Help! A blizzard has caught you off-guard while outside in the open countryside. Gusts of biting wind cut through everything as freezing snow swirls all around. How will you survive this?

SURVIVE STEP-BY-STEP

SNOW TRENCH SHELTER

1 Stop and don't try and walk through the blizzard: you'll just get lost. Instead get out your shovel and dig a shelter.

2 Dig a trench with a wall at the top against the wind. Use branches to help construct the wall and pack the snow down by stomping on it.

3 Remove heavy outer clothing while digging to reduce sweating. Sweat will make you cold after you have finished digging.

4 Lie down in your shelter and cover yourself with blankets or light branches if available. These will allow you to breathe while the snow falls. Stand up every 20 minutes to shake off the snow so you do not become buried.

FROSTBITE AND HYPOTHERMIA

Frostbite and hypothermia are serious medical conditions that can lead to the loss of fingers and toes and even death. Move your limbs, warm yourself as quickly as possible and seek medical help if you display the following symptoms:

FROSTBITE:

- numbness
- tingling
- burning or itching fingers and toes
- Hard white skin that becomes yellowish and then black

HYPOTHERMIA:

- slurred speech
- loss of coordination and bladder control
- stiff joints
- puffy face
- mental confusion

CASE STUDY

In 1972, the deadliest blizzard in history struck Iran and left 4,000 dead. The blizzard blew for nearly a week, snapping powerlines, burying villages and leaving the west of the country under several metres of snow. Those who lived had to survive for several days in -25°C (-13°F) temperatures without water, food or electricity. Then, there was only a period of a few days for rescuers to find survivors before another blizzard set in.

Tehran

IRAN

LANDSLIDES

A landslide is the massive movement of rock, debris and earth down a mountainside, cliff or slope. Landslides can happen slowly over time or suddenly at terrifying speeds. A landslide can hurtle down a slope at 320 km/h (200 mph) and sweep away people, roads and towns in its path.

Tell me about landslides

WHAT MAKES A LANDSLIDE?

A landslide begins when the materials forming a slope can no longer resist the force of gravity. So what makes these materials slide down a slope?

HOW A LANDSLIDE FORMS

A landslide can start for several different reasons. The most common ones are:

- **NATURAL FORCES:** earthquakes, volcanic eruptions and storms can trigger a landslide. Heavy rainfall and snow can also saturate a slope until it is so heavy that it slides forwards.

- **EROSION:** changes in a slope's rock formation or the vegetation growing on it can weaken the slope and cause a landslide.

- **HUMAN ACTIVITY:** removing trees, digging soil to sow crops or building houses on a slope can all destabilize it and bring about a landslide.

Deforested slopes often cause landslides.

MENACING MUDFLOWS

A mudflow is one of the deadliest types of landslide. Mudflows develop when rock, earth and other debris becomes mixed with water to form a river of mud. This commonly occurs after heavy rainfall or a rapid snow melt. Mudflows often strike without warning and travel at tremendous speeds, picking up trees and boulders as they rush downhill.

Mudflows can travel for several kilometres downhill before burying people, cars and villages at the bottom.

In 1958, a magnitude 7.9 earthquake triggered a landslide in Alaska's Lituya Bay that caused a 30 m (98 ft.) high tsunami wave.

UNDERWATER LANDSLIDES

Earthquakes and underwater volcanoes can sometimes cause landslides to occur under the sea. Called submarine landslides, these can bring about a massive displacement of water. When this water is pushed upwards and out, it can form a tsunami. A landslide on a cliff or slope by a lake can also cause a tsunami.

CASE STUDY

One of the world's largest landslides took place during the 1980 eruption of Mount St Helens, a volcano in Washington's Cascade Mountains, USA. The eruption blew 400 m (1,300 ft.) off the top of the volcano and sent 2.8 cubic kilometres (0.67 cubic miles) of material hurtling down its mountainside. This flattened whole forests below, destroyed over 200 houses and caused the deaths of 57 people.

How to prepare

HOW TO PREPARE

Landslides can be sudden and unexpected, but follow these steps to be as forewarned as possible.

STEP 1

HAVE A PLAN

If you live below a landslide-prone slope, then it is vital to have an evacuation plan that you practise with your family. This will ensure you all know where to go and what to do if a landslide strikes.

STEP 2

HAVE AN EMERGENCY KIT

A landslide may mean you are buried beneath debris and cut off from the world for days or even weeks. Assembling an emergency kit (see pages 12–13) in advance is therefore essential.

STEP 3

PROTECT YOUR HOME

Planting trees to make slopes more stable, or to create a debris barrier, is a good first step. Digging channels for landslides to travel down is another way of preparing. Often landslides strike the same place over and over again, so it should be obvious where to dig.

STEP 4

WATCH FOR SIGNS

Small changes in a slope often indicate that something bigger is coming. Little landslides, cracks in the ground or toppled trees can all show that a slope is unstable. Monitor your slope closely!

HOW TO SURVIVE

It started with the sound of trees cracking and boulders knocking together. Now a landslide is speeding down the slope towards you. What do you do?

SURVIVE STEP-BY-STEP

1 Move away from the landslide as quickly as possible. Remember: a mudflow can travel faster than you can run or walk!

2 If escaping in a car, don't cross a river or through moving water on a road. Many people die this way during landslides.

3 If you are inside, move to the strongest room in the centre of the house. Shelter under a table and hold on!

4 If you are caught in a landslide and all else fails, curl into a tight ball and protect your head and neck with your arms.

5 Don't go back! Even if it seems like a landslide is finished, there may be more debris on the way. Wait until authorities have given the all-clear on the radio.

TEST YOUR MATES

Ok, you've survived the landslide and have come out unscathed. Now, you're a landslide veteran. Why not test your knowledge with this true or false quiz?

A Pets such as cats and dogs can sense a landslide days before it strikes. **T/F**

B Stream water changing from clear to muddy may indicate a landslide is on its way. **T/F**

C Replanting land damaged by landslides can help reduce further erosion. **T/F**

D Landslides do not occur during the night. **T/F**

E Always take your pets along if you are ordered to evacuate from a landslide. **T/F**

LANDSLIDES ON MARS?

The largest landslide scientists know about took place on Mars. Billions of years ago, an asteroid crashed into the planet and caused its smooth, northern hemisphere to be separated from its rocky, southern hemisphere. This caused a mass of land the size of the United States to slide downwards and create an area known as Arabia Terra.

Answers are at the back of the book

93

HEATWAVES

Heatwaves are long periods of unusually hot weather that can pose a great threat to human life. Normally occurring during the summer, a heatwave can last for several weeks and bring temperatures that cause illness and death. Thousands lose their lives to heatwaves every year.

Tell me about heatwaves

WHAT MAKES A HEATWAVE?

A heatwave may mean lots of hot weather for a long time. But why is this so dangerous? And what causes a heatwave to form in the first place?

HOW A HEATWAVE FORMS

Heatwaves are formed by trapped, warm air near the Earth's surface. This occurs when a high pressure weather system forces air downwards. The force of this pressure acts like a lid over the warm air near the ground. Without rising air, there is no rain and nothing to stop the air from getting hotter. This is when conditions are perfect for a heatwave to strike.

Hot, humid air lingering over populated areas can cause many human casualties.

DEFINING HEATWAVES

Everyone has a different idea about when hot weather becomes a heatwave. Some countries define a heatwave as 'five or more days with a temperature of 5°C (9°F) higher than the average for that time of year'. In Australia, a heatwave is defined by five or more days with temperatures over 35°C (95°F), or three days or more with temperatures over 40°C (104°F).

In India, a heatwave is defined by temperatures that are 5 to 6°C (9 to 10.8°F) higher than normal.

HEATWAVE EFFECTS

The effects of high temperatures can be lethal for the human body. This is especially true when there is also humidity (water vapour in the air). High humidity means the air is already saturated with water and our sweat won't evaporate, making us hotter. This can lead to a condition called hyperthermia, which is an excess of body heat. Hyperthermia can lead to heat stroke, a life-threatening condition where a person's body temperature reaches 40°C (104°F) or more.

CLIMATE CHANGE

The frequency and intensity of heatwaves are increasing as a result of global warming brought about by climate change. In 2018, scientists found that climate change has doubled the chances of heatwaves occurring worldwide. This will make severe heatwaves a common event by the 2040s. It is also predicted that heatwaves will put 48 per cent of the world's population at risk of heat-related illness or death by 2100.

48% of deaths

How to prepare

HOW TO PREPARE

The temperature's rising and it's getting harder to cope...
Follow these four steps to keep your cool in a heatwave.

STEP 1

STAY INSIDE

Organise your day so you are outside as little as possible between 11am and 3pm. Especially avoid sports and exercise at this time, or anything else that might make you hot.

STEP 2

STOCKPILE LIQUIDS

Get ready to stay hydrated. Keep bottles or jugs of water in the fridge and eat hydrating foods such as watermelon, lettuce, cucumber and strawberries.

STEP 3

A COMFORTABLE HOME

Keep your house cool by drawing curtains against the sun. Put your sheets in the freezer a few hours before bed to help you get to sleep. You can try putting your underwear in there too (but only if they're clean)!

STEP 4

OUTSIDE WEAR

Wear loose, light clothing when you are outside and a hat to keep off the sun. Learn to love shorts, flip flops and straw hats.

How to endure

HOW TO ENDURE

There has been no rain for weeks, the temperature is off the scale, and it's too hot to sleep at night. You're in a heatwave! So, what can you do to survive it?

HELP, I'M TOO HOT!

 Start and end your day with a cold shower or bath. It may feel strange at first, but it will bring down your body temperature to cope with the heat.

 Drink at least two litres of liquid a day. Cool water is best, but smoothies and fruit juices are also good. Avoid tea, coffee and sugary drinks.

 Keep you and your pets inside during the hottest part of the day. You can help cool pets down by inviting them to lie on a cold towel from the freezer.

 Stay out of the sun and if you need to go out plan your trip with breaks in air-conditioned buildings, such as public libraries.

 Monitor yourself and your family for early signs of hyperthermia. These are dizziness, weakness, a rapid pulse and coordination problems. If someone stops sweating, seems confused, or faints, seek medical help immediately.

CASE STUDY

In 2003, Europe experienced one of its deadliest heatwaves in history. The heatwave made up one of the hottest European summers since 1540 and caused the deaths of over 30,000 people. More than 14,000 people died of heat stroke and dehydration in France alone, where temperatures topped 40°C (104°F) for over seven days running. Climate change is believed to be one of the main factors involved in the severity of the heatwave.

? TEST YOUR MATES

So, you've survived the heat and rain is forecast. Congratulations, you are a DIY heatwave survivor! Now test your knowledge with this true or false quiz.

A Many people die during a heatwave from drowning while swimming.　　T/F

B Dehydration is serious, but humans can survive for three weeks without water.　　T/F

C Air pollution is one of the main killers during a heatwave.　　T/F

D Long heatwaves often lead to drought and the loss of crops.　　T/F

E Around 30 per cent of the world's population live in places that deliver over 20 days of deadly temperatures a year.　　T/F

Answers are at the back of the book

DROUGHTS

A drought occurs when there has been no rain in a region for a long period. This can lead to severe water shortages, crop failure and famine. Over time, drought can destroy whole communities and lead to large-scale, forced migration. Widespread death and illness often accompany long-term droughts.

Tell me about droughts

WHAT MAKES A DROUGHT?

Droughts are not as sudden as many other natural disasters. A severe drought can take years or even decades to develop. So why do they form?

HOW A DROUGHT FORMS

A drought is created when more water is being evaporated from the ground than is falling in rainfall. This lack of rain causes plants and crops to die and the soil to dry out. Over time, water levels in lakes and reservoirs fall and the water flow in streams and rivers declines. This can lead to water shortages. If the dry weather continues, a drought forms.

Droughts can cause desertification: the process that makes once fertile land desert-like.

HEATWAVES AND DROUGHTS

A heatwave (see pages 94–101) is a period of little rain and high temperatures, which can often lead to a drought. A drought can then lead to more heat. This is because when there is no water in the ground for the Sun to evaporate, it heats up the land and air instead. This heat then adds to the drought conditions, which creates a cycle.

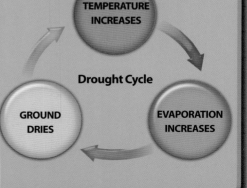

Drought Cycle

TEMPERATURE INCREASES

EVAPORATION INCREASES

GROUND DRIES

HUMAN CAUSES

Human activity can help trigger droughts. Deforestation, or cutting down trees, prevents soil from holding water and causes it to dry out. Changing the path of a river or stream or building a dam can also lead to drought. This is because it restricts the flow of water to one area and leaves the rest of the region to dry out.

A dam can often cause a drought to occur on the previously watered plains below it.

DROUGHT IMPACT

Droughts have many serious impacts. These can include:

- The failure of crops and farms, followed by food shortages.

- The drying-up of lakes, rivers and streams, destroying the habitats of aquatic animals.

- The outbreak of wildfires, caused by extreme dry conditions and high temperatures.

- A lack of water for drinking, sanitation and to keep crops alive.

- The large migration of people away from a drought-stricken area to survive.

How to prepare

HOW TO PREPARE

You've read the signs. A drought seems likely. Now, this is what you're going to do...

STEP 1

CONSERVE WATER

Never pour water down the drain, but instead use it to water plants. Take shorter showers. Don't flush the toilet unless there is solid waste to go down.

STEP 2

COLLECT WATER

Buy a large water tank and place it under the main guttering downpipe at your home. This water can be used for plants and bathing, but don't drink it!

STEP 3

STOCKPILE WATER

The possibility of a long drought may cause supplies of bottled water to run out, so make sure you buy yours early. Plan for 4 litres (1 gallon) of water per day for each person in your house.

STEP 4

MAKE WATER CHOICES

Your house plants and lawn look good, but they won't hydrate or feed you. Use your precious water supply for people and crops first!

HOW TO SURVIVE

There's been no rain for weeks. The ground outside is parched and cracked. It's hot, dry and there's no water anywhere. How will you survive this dreadful drought?

HELP, I'M THIRSTY!

Because we cannot cause the sky to rain, droughts are beyond our control. The best option is to accept a drought is happening and learn to endure it.

1 Find new ways of conserving water. Don't leave the tap on while brushing your teeth. Do your dishes in a plastic bowl not a dishwasher. Only wash every other day. Keep a bucket in the shower to collect water for plants.

2 Add mulch to the soil where crops are planted. Mulch can be made up of anything that retains water, including straw, bark, compost, old carpet and orange peel.

6 If you're searching for water in the wild, look out for animals and follow them to a water source. Animals sometimes become violent during droughts, so be on your guard.

3 Wildfires are a real risk during droughts. Keep your eyes peeled for signs of smoke and listen to the news for wildfire warnings.

4 Make sure you drink between 1 and 2 litres (0.25 and 0.5 gallons) of water every day. Drink the water you need to stay alive!

5 If you are lost outside during a drought make sure you only move early in the morning and late in the afternoon, when temperatures are cooler. Beware of pools of water with no vegetation around them – this is a sign the water is contaminated.

DEADLIEST DROUGHT

One of the deadliest droughts in history struck northern China between 1876 and 1879. During the drought there was almost no rainfall and most crops failed. This led to widespread famine and the deaths of 13 million people through starvation. By the time the rains returned in 1879, the affected regions of Shanxi, Azhili, Henan and Shandong had been largely depopulated.

TRUE OR FALSE

You're conserving water, staying healthy and even managing a shower now and then. Congratulations – you are a drought survivor! Now test your knowledge with this quiz.

A Droughts can still occur during long periods of heavy rain. **T/F**

B Sometimes weeks and months can pass before it is clear a drought is occurring. **T/F**

C Scientists can predict when a drought is going to happen. **T/F**

D The 'Dust Bowl' was a devastating 1930s drought in America. **T/F**

Answers are at the back of the book

TEST YOUR MATES
? ANSWERS

EARTHQUAKES

A: True   B: False   C: False   D: False   E: True   F: False   G: True

AVALANCHES

A: True   B: True   C: False   D: True   E: False   F: True

FLASH FLOODS

A: True   B: False   C: True   D: False   E: True   F: True

VOLCANOES

A: True   B: True   C: False   D: True

TORNADOES

A: True   B: True   C: True

WILDFIRES

A: True   B: True   C: False   D: False   E: True

LANDSLIDES

A: False   B: True   C: True   D: False   E: True

HEATWAVES

A: True   B: False   C: True   D: True   E: True

DROUGHTS

A: False   B: True   C: False   D: True

GLOSSARY

Asteroid A rocky object in Space that ranges in size from smaller than a car to 1,000 km (600 mi.) across.

Atmosphere The layers of gases around the Earth made up of nitrogen, oxygen, water vapour and other gases.

Climate change The average weather conditions of the entire planet over a long period of time. Scientists believe the Earth's climate has been rapidly getting warmer.

Evaporation The process where liquids change to a gas or vapour. Sweat drying from your body is an example of evaporation.

Famine A severe shortage of food – people in a famine may die from extreme hunger or disease.

Frostbite Damage to the skin from freezing temperatures – usually the fingers and toes.

Hemisphere The Earth is divided into two halves – the Northern and Southern Hemispheres. The line dividing the two is called the equator.

Hydration The process of making your body take in water. To stay hydrated you must drink plenty of water. When you aren't drinking enough you can become dehydrated.

Hypothermia A dangerous drop in body temperature caused by exposure to cold temperatures. Normal body temperature is around 37°C (98.6°F), hypothermia occurs when your body temperature falls below 35°C (95°F).

INDEX